Analysis Father , Poor Father, of Robert Kiyosaki

Table of Contents

Introduction

This book tells the story of a person (the narrator and author) who has two fathers: his biological father, the poor dad, and the other, the father of his best friend from childhood, Mike; the rich dad, both taught the author how to be successful, but through very different approaches. To the author, it was clear that his father's approach was more financially meaningful. Throughout the book, the author compares both fathers: their principles, ideas, financial activities, their degree of dynamism and how his true father, the poor and yet combative one, but who is highly educated, fears his rich dad due to his properties and eye for business.

The author compares his poor dad with those who run around constantly seeking success, trapped in a vicious circle of needs, but they'll never be able to satisfy their dreams of wealth due to an obvious lack: financial education. They spend a lot of time in school, studying the problems of the world, but they haven't learned any useful lessons about money, simply because this lesson is never taught in school.

On the other hand, his rich dad represents the independent core of the company, which is deliberately based on corporate power, as well as on their personal knowledge of taxes and accounting (or that of their financial advisors) who manipulate it in their favor.

The subject of the book is reduced to two fundamental concepts: a positive attitude and a fearless entrepreneurial spirit. The author focuses on these two concepts by providing several examples for each, and emphasizes on the need for financial education, explaining how corporate power helps enrich the rich, monitoring their activity, overcoming obstacles by not promoting laziness, as well as other negative attitudes, and recognizing human characteristics and the way in which their preconceived ideas and education hinder their financial freedom goals.

The author presents six main lessons, which he discusses throughout the book:

Rich people don't work for money.

The importance of financial education.

Your own company

Taxes and partnerships.

The rich make money.

The need to work to learn and not to work for money.

Character summaries.

Rich Dad, Poor Dad revolves around three main characters: the poor dad, the rich dad (Kiyosaki's second father) and his son (the author himself as the book's narrator). Each character's essence is:

Poor dad, educated but lacking street smarts.

Rich dad - very little education (eighth grade), having learned a lot through life.

Kiyosaki: the spectator who learns from both experiences but only assumes the characteristics of the rich dad.

Poor dad.

The author compares his father to the millions of fathers who encourage their children to succeed in school so they can get a good job at a good company. His father believed in the traditional principles of hard work, saving money and buying unsustainable material goods. He felt that everyone should aspire to get a good job in a solid company, which is why he's disappointed when his son leaves his job at a great and respectable company.

The poor dad thinks that education is the passport to success. He has a doctorate and attended Ivy League universities, but's always experienced financial difficulties. He believed he'd never be a rich man, and the author points out that this has become a self-fulfilling prophecy. The poor dad was more interested in a good education than in money. The author wrote that his father would always say: "I'm not interested in money" or "money does not matter".

The author notes that his father worried more about issues such as job security and social security, vacations and holidays, company insurance, raises and promotions. The author felt that his father was more interested in these factors than in the work itself. That's what the author calls being trapped in the race to success. His father worked hard but, in one way or another, never achieved financial progress. The poor dad's money-based approached was based on the fact that he had to work hard to get enough money to pay the bills (as opposed to the rich dad who raised money for himself).

Rich dad

The author wrote that when he was nine years old, he understood that his rich dad was much more logical than his poor dad. It's from the rich dad that the author learned not to say "I can't afford that", but rather ask himself: "How can I afford that?" He explains this principle by sharing an incident from when he and his best friend Mike went to work for Mike's father. The rich dad voluntarily paid them very low wages to anger them and create a feeling of injustice, to make sure they knew that to progress they needed to work for themselves and not for others.

For example, in this part of the book, where the author complains to the rich dad because he can hardly buy him anything with his salary, the rich dad tells him that he shouldn't insist on the fact that his wages are low, but instead ask "how can I earn more" because this encourages the brain to act. The rich dad says that when someone says "I can't afford it", his brain stops working. It kills initiatives and promotes passivity.

The author adds that, even though his poor dad had invested time and effort in education, he didn't know about investments. However, his rich dad was very adept at investments, because that was everything he did. His father's attitude towards money manifested itself in the adage "lack of money is the root of all evil" (his poor dad, on the other hand, believed that the love of money was the root of all evil).

According to the author, his rich dad also supported the idea that taxes punished producers and rewarded non-producers. He was the one who encouraged speeches at the table and who was presented by the author as someone who'd learned to manage risk instead of taking them.

The son (Robert T. Kiyosaki)

The author begins his book, Rich Dad, Poor Dad, by saying that was lucky to have had two fathers. He learned valuable lessons from both, but in the first chapter, it became clear that the father had the most money-sensitive approach. He compares and contrasts both father's opinions on hard work, study, savings and investment, and notices how different the rich and the poor's habits are. He attributes his financial wisdom to the many conversations he had with his rich dad.

The author adopts a sensible approach towards money and underlines the need for knowing about accounting so that the reader can clearly understand assets and liabilities. He creates simple diagrams that show cash inflows and outflows, as well as how the rich build an asset column and the poor a responsibility (expenses) column. It's obvious that the author grants more importance to know about accounting, no matter how boring it may be, because he says that it's "the most important subject of his life".

The author transmits his messages effectively through his numerous examples and anecdotes, thus revealing his pro-capitalist position.

The author also shows his understanding of the mechanisms used by the government and tax authorities and concludes that it's the middle class that pays for the poor. The rich barely pay taxes because they know how to use tax legislation to their advantage.

Summaries of the chapters.

Chapter 1: Rich dad, Poor dad.

The story of Robert Kiyosaki and Mike begins in 1956, in Hawaii, when both children were nine years old. His first enrichment program was a counterfeit nickel production company. They made nickel plaster casts and cast lead toothpaste tubes and filled the molds to produce nickel. Their project ended when Mike's father informed the children of their illegal activity.

After that day, the children spent their free time studying finance and economics with Mike's father, the rich dad. Mike's father's first lesson was his hatred for the "rat race". He shared it by forcing the children to work in one of his grocery stores for three hours with a salary of ten cents per hour. A few weeks later, Kiyosaki, tired of being exploited, asked him for a raise, but Mike's father reduced his salary and told him to work for free. In the end, both children, tired of feeling undervalued (and not being paid), met individually with Mike's father. During their meetings with a rich dad, he apologized for their lack of payment and offered them either a moral lesson or a raise. Both children chose to learn the moral lesson, even though the rich dad had offered them a raise.

He started with twenty-five cents, one dollar, two dollars and even five dollars, which would have been considered a large sum of money for one hour of work, but the boys stood firm in their decision to learn the lesson. The lesson they had to learn was on the "race to success", instead of spending their whole lives getting some money in their pockets and a lot of money in someone else's pocket, ask others to work hard so you can get money in your pocket.

Of all the lessons the children learned, this was the most important one. (Kiyosaki and Lechter 28-35)

Chapter 2: Rich people don't work for money.

The author tells his readers to forget the notion that life is a teacher. He says: "The only thing that life does is push you"

This chapter is about people who feel more comfortable playing it safe because they haven't been taught to take risks early in life. The author expands on the idea that the poor and the middle classes work for money, fear and greed and that these are the causes of ignorance and poverty, and on the importance of using emotions instead of emotional thinking.

The author also states that opportunities come and go in life; the rich recognize them instantly and turn them into gold bars. Others don't see these opportunities because they're too busy looking for money and safety. As the author says, "that's all they'll get."

Chapter 3: Why teach financial education?

Kiyosaki and Mike's story continues later in life, in 1990, and both, who are now adults, have made incredible progress in terms of finances and socioeconomic status. Mike was able to take his father's lesson and apply it to his life. He took control of his father's large company and expanded every aspect of the empire. He's currently raising his son to take control of the retired company. As for Kiyosaki, he was able to retire at 47 with his wife Kim. During a meeting at the Edgewater Beach Hotel in Chicago, Charles Schwab, Samuel Insull, Howard Hopson, Ivar Kreuger, Leon Frazier, Richard Whitney, Arthur Cotton, Jesse Livermore and Albert Fall met to discuss various investments and financial projects. Twenty-five years later, a report indicated that most of the extremely rich people who'd gathered in Chicago had ended up in jail, dead or broke. The main idea to remember from the outcome of these unfortunate entrepreneurs is that one needs to master financial education to stay safe.

The idea shown by the great entrepreneurs of the 20s still prevails, with some professional athletes who make bad financial decisions and end up with almost nothing.

This specific lesson is designed to teach people not to use their money wisely once they have it, but to be smart with their money before they even get it. Basically, don't try to build a skyscraper or even a house without first building a solid foundation. According to Kiyosaki, one single rule can help people establish a solid foundation. Know the difference between a resource and a responsibility and make sure to only verify your resources. (Kiyosaki and Lechter 56)

In this chapter, the author supports the author's financial independence. It's based on the idea that money buys freedom, as well as the chance to retire without the fear of surviving. He says: "Intelligence solves problems and makes money. Money without financial information is money that will soon leave."

The author believes that financial education begins with practical knowledge of accounting. One needs to know the difference between assets and liabilities.

To make these two terms understandable to the reader, the author draws a rudimentary diagram of both concepts to motivate the reader to buy assets to consolidate the asset column, keeping liabilities (expenses) to a minimum. The author claims that the poor remain poor because they do the opposite. Their liabilities accumulate and they have no assets, so their balance sheets and income statements don't balance each other. People should understand that this isn't what they earn, but what they keep, according to their author, and that's a key principle for this chapter.

Chapter 4: Take care of your business.

In this chapter, the author slowly introduces the concept of real estate investments, and uses McDonald's as an example. Note that McDonald's may not be the best burger in the world, but it has the "most beautiful

intersections and roads in the United States".
The author states that people should worry
about their business if they want to be
financially independent. They shouldn't
interfere in their employer's business, they
should strive to find a way to become their
own leader and develop their own business.

The author continues his discussion with
asset constitution. For him, real assets are
the ones that have value: stocks, bonds,
mutual funds, real estate that generates an
income, tickets, intellectual property
royalties, etc.

This chapter also reveals the author's
investment preferences: real estate and
shares. For real estate, he says that he starts

little by little, exchanging his properties for larger ones, and then delays paying capital gain taxes through an IRS mechanism.

Chapter 5: Tax History and Corporate Power

The author states that the poor allow large machines (companies) to manipulate them, while the rich know how to work the large machines. This means that the rich know how to use the power of society to protect and improve their assets. A company's advantage over that of an individual lies in the way companies pay taxes, according to the author.

To clarify this point: people make money, they pay taxes on that money, and live with what's left. Companies, on the other hand, earn money, spend everything they can and pay taxes on what's left.

The author adds that individuals may not know how manipulated they are; they work from January to mid-May to enrich the government by paying income taxes. Meanwhile, the rich barely pay taxes.

The author recommends developing one's financial IQ to get out of the banality of everyday life. This is achieved by acquiring knowledge in accounting, investment, market and law. He says that being ignorant makes you feel bad, while being informed means "you have the chance to fight".

Chapter 6: The Rich Inventor

The author develops the concept of insecurity. He says that every person is born with talent, but that talent is eliminated due to doubts and insecurities. He points out that it isn't necessarily people with a good education who progress, they are just bold and adventurous. "People never progress financially, even if they have a lot of money, because they have chances they can't take advantage of", he says. Most of them sit waiting for opportunities. The author's idea is that people create their own luck; they shouldn't wait for it. He says it's the same with money. It must be created.

In this chapter, the author analyzes the importance of education (even though some critics say he seems to minimize its importance). The author makes it clear that "a trained mind is a rich mind". In his analysis, there are two types of investors, each of whom has a different mindset: those who opt for pre-packaged investments and those who make investments based on their needs. Their goals.

The author encourages people to hire smarter people than themselves because, by capitalizing on other people's knowledge, an intelligent individual builds his own knowledge, and therefore, has more power over those who don't have it.

Chapter 7: Learn to learn, not work for money.

In this chapter the author talks about the skills that individuals need to develop to be financially successful.

The reader is given an example, of a young woman with a master's degree in English literature who is offended when someone suggests learning to sell and do direct marketing. After all her efforts to obtain her diploma, she didn't think she'd have to lower herself so much as to have to learn to become a saleswoman, a profession that didn't demand much. The author uses this example to state that people need to learn various skills in the path to financial freedom.

The author mentions management skills. He says that people need to know how to manage their cash flow, systems and workforce. This helps you gain sales and marketing skills. He also focuses on communication skills. He says that a lot of people have a scientific inclination, and therefore powerful knowledge, but fail miserably in communications. These people have a "skill that is far from great wealth".

The author draws attention to a surprising aspect of great rich families: they give money, abundantly, unlike the poor who believe that charity begins at home.

Chapter 8: Overcoming obstacles.

The author believes that five main personality traits hinder the human being: fear, cynicism, laziness, bad habits, arrogance. He explains that, while it's normal to be afraid, the important thing is to know how to deal with it. The author shares his feelings about this particular predilection with Texas and Texans: "When they win, they win big and when they lose, they do so spectacularly."

The author affirms that it isn't a matter of balance, but FOCUS. He recommends ignoring the little problems of the world.

That only consists of worrying about the sky falling and spending the rest of one's life in pessimism. He says he constantly hears people saying that they want to be rich, but when he suggests money form real estate, their first reaction is "I don't want to fix toilets". The author thinks that it's ironic how they are more concerned with anecdotes, such as fixing toilets, that with what is happening in real estate. In conclusion, the author says that it's healthy to be greedy – greedy – greedy; when a decision is made, the person should always wonder: "How does that benefit me?"

Chapter 9: Introduction

This chapter consists of suggestions to create and create personal wealth. His first advice is to find a reason greater than reality to motivate you. What he means by this, is to awaken the financial genius in oneself by empowering one's spirit. He says that people need to have a strong purpose/life.

The next tip is to feed the spirit. By nurturing the mind, the author states that people acquire the power of choice.

The author also advises people to choose their friends carefully. He says he avoids people who constantly proclaim that the sky is falling, and instead encourages readers to spend time with people who like to talk about money because they can have valuable lessons to share. The author also believes that people should study a field and then learn a new one, although it's important to choose what you'll study.

Here's another suggestion that the author states people don't practice: they need to be paid first. Even if the money runs out, people need to be paid first. That goes hand in hand with the effective management of three things: money, people and personal time.

The author also suggests being generous. He thinks it makes sense to pay his agent, because he's his ally, and "his eyes and ears in the market."

The author suggests having heroes. They're indispensable in life because they not only inspire you, they also make it easier. They stimulate the human mind to think: "If they can do it, why not me?"

Another piece of advice that the author shares is "teach and receive". His words speak loudly about this idea: "Some powers in this world are much smarter than us".

You can do it yourself, but it's easier to do it with the help of existing powers. All you have to be is generous with what you have and the powers will be generous with you.

Chapter 10: Still want more? Here are some things you can do.

This chapter is a kind of complement to the previous chapter. It gives readers additional tips to help them get financial rewards. One tip is to stop doing what you're doing if it no longer works or isn't viable. The author encourages readers to look for new ideas, to pick the brains of experienced people who've already achieved what each one aspires to do.

He recommends keeping the learning curve alive by taking classes, buying audio lessons, attending seminars.

When looking for real estate investment opportunities, the author recommends searching in the right places. One way to do this is to go for a run in the neighborhood you're interested in.

People can acquire real estate even if they don't have sufficient funds for the down payment. In fact, with a bit of intelligence, the author says that people can even earn money without capital.

Well, this happened one day. After going over my previous article, Rebuilding Robert Kiyosaki, it became inevitable to review his famous book on personal finance, Rich dad, Poor dad. This book has inspired many people, but it also seems to have attracted many strong critics. And upon writing this review, I'm reading this book for the third time. I thought it might be interesting to immediately mention the first two times I read the book and my reactions after reading it.

The first time I read the book, I felt inspired. I wanted to implement some of the book's ideas, but what I discovered is that you simply can't follow these steps, spend five hours searching and starting with € 60,000 in cash to buy properties.

Many people have been disappointed by this. In the end, I found a long negative analysis of John T. Reed's RDPD and I was almost surprised by the amount of criticism he had. After this review, I read the book a second time and concluded that it was a waste of time. Not long after the second time I read it, a reader asked me to write what I thought of the author, who wrote many similar books.

So what sort of book could cause such a mind-shift? Rich dad, poor dad is what I would call a personal finance perspective shaped as a parable, much like a book I read before, The Wealthy Barber. But while The Wealthy Barber has essentially associated its base of how one handles personal money in a parable with examples that can be sought and solved directly and independently, Rich

Dad, Poor Dad, makes one completely rethink the use of money.

For example, instead of considering an asset as a valuable element, this book defines an asset as an element that generates cash flows. This means that, according to this book, your home is not an asset.

Now I read this book for a third time, without the cynicism that was inherent in my last reading of the book. I will also limit my observations to what is on the book cover (that is, I will set aside the author's external perspectives) and accept the parable of the rich dad for what it is, a parable. I'm only interested in the following question: Are personal finance earnings included in these covers?

Six lessons learned

The title Rich Dad, Poor Dad, refers to Robert's two main male influences during his childhood. His father, the figurative "poor dad", worked in a stable job, while the "rich dad" (his friend's father) ran various businesses. Most of this book is told from Robert's point of view, who's taught how to make money by his "rich dad", and sees his "poor dad" make huge mistakes with money.

The first two-thirds of the book covers six lessons that Robert learned from his rich dad.

1. Rich people don't work for money.

The importance of financial education.

Your own company

Taxes and partnerships.

The rich make money.

The need to work to learn and not to work for money.

1.-This lesson has an ambiguous title that gives you two different meanings, depending on how you read it, in fact, depending on where you focus. If you read the title as rich people don't work for money, it gives you the wrong lesson. The rich work, and they work hard enough. The title should be read as the rich shouldn't work for money. They work to learn things and the things they learn can be easily applied to earn money over and over again. I totally agree with this feeling: good ideas are always more valuable than good work, because you can continue to take advantage of good ideas, while doing a good job.

Another part of this lesson that I liked is that the "rich dad" is actually quite thrifty. Even though he has a lot of money in the bank, he drives a cheap car and doesn't live in a villa.

Too many people are extremely rich in material things, so I appreciate how it shows that being rich often has very little to do with material goods.

Being rich means not having to worry about paying your bills, it doesn't mean driving a sports car (well, not at least you can pay for it in cash on not sweat about it).

2. Why teach financial education?

This part of the book was highly controversial. Basically, this chapter redefines the term asset. For the most part, an asset is something valuable. For example, your home is an asset because you own it and it's valuable.

Well, this section of the book redefines that word. For Robert Kiyosaki, an asset is something that generates an income, while a liability is anything that has costs. In other words, according to this definition, your home isn't an asset, but a responsibility.

It may have a monetary value, but it doesn't generate an income. Instead, assets are forms of passive income that you control, such as rental property or intellectual property.

So, what's the general lesson here? Basically, you get rich by accumulating assets, as defined in this book.

This means that my car generates expenses and isn't a good investment because it's expensive and I have to pay for it for years, while if you invest in a property that generates a monthly rent, in which the mortgage expenses are covered and some money is left, it makes it a good asset.

Wealth comes from having enough assets to generate enough income to cover all your expenses, while you have money left to invest in more assets.

3.Take care of your business.

This chapter's main subject is that a person with good financial health should spend his free time not spending his salary, but investing it in businesses as much as possible (as defined in this book). This is another lesson with which I completely agree: pay off debts and start investing as soon as possible in income-generating activities. This lesson was short and very productive.

4. Tax History and Corporate Power

This is the section of the book that made me stop believing in the ideas presented. First, after discussing all the steps of the rather frugal example of the "rich dad", Kiyosaki begins to describe a lifestyle, in which he buys a luxury car and the sort. What? This doesn't go with the previous lessons.

What's even worse, is that this chapter misrepresents several basic facts about taxes, of which I'm perfectly aware, because my father owned a business and paid taxes. First, if one starts declaring expenses such as a luxury car as a necessary business expense, will they accept it? There's a big difference between creating a personal company and buying a company vehicle to use with that company, but that's the idea, which is very clear, it's is rational to spend it to avoid taxes when buying a luxury car. One may be able to justify a business jet for traveling, but why does a company need a luxury car?

Kiyosaki mentions several tax deductions in this chapter, but most of them aren't deductions at all, they're just fiscal delays. In almost every case, one must keep an asset until it dies or racks up a monstrous tax bill. If you play your tax cards well, you can deduct a large number of bills and pay the minimum allowed, which makes it more difficult for an employee or self-employed person.

Keeping money within a corporate structure as an individual has some advantages, but it's primarily to minimize taxes on reasonable expenses, those related to the money one earns regardless of their job. This doesn't mean that a company can magically buy a luxury car.

5.The rich inventor of money.

The author tells the story of an incredibly good real estate transaction that ended up in "court", in which Kiyosaki claims to have earned $ 40,000 in five hours. At the time we live in, these numbers aren't commonly used, or the time of five-hour for earning such revenues, these times aren't true for in real estate, sales times and profits are much larger and have more risks, having more advertising methods and connecting with potential customers greatly improves the sales process, but don't think you'll get quick and easy results, pursuing such short-term results can bring great economic problems.

This doesn't aim to criticize this chapter's general lesson; you can invest money, however, the easiest way to earn money in today's arena is to create your own intellectual property. With the Internet, there are many ways to distribute and monetize intellectual property: sell crafts you create, create websites based on your ideas, sell your music or presentations.

6. Learn to work – Don't work for money

In this section, we need to be clear about Kiyosaki's idea, most people are in a hamster wheel, but many of them have been driven there by their families, education and acquaintances, also by society, and they have two options, to realize their situation, open their eyes and change it, if their current life frustrates them, otherwise they can continue on this path.

Everyone should strive to learn as much as possible when they work, as this could transform their understanding of the world and perhaps even develop methods to open their own business and become independent.

However, it's ridiculous to despise people who choose to work and live like "hamsters". Is Jack Welch a "hamster"? He was hired by General Electric for forty years.

Arguments in rich dad, poor dad.

One issue that emerged from this book is that to be rich, an individual must aspire to have a production system or the means to produce, instead of working for another individual. The author notes that there's obviously something confusing about being an employee; it closes your mind to other possibilities and halts any initiative.

Financial intelligence is the most powerful resource. By studying accounting and investment precepts, the author believes that people will be able to see the difference between an asset and a liability; actually, this is the book's most concrete point, learning the right application and not generating a chain of expenses, which is a bad thing, while gathering assets is a good thing.

Conclusion

Unlike people who make money and then pay taxes on what they earn, companies earn, spend what they want to spend and pay taxes on what's left. Companies, therefore, have a certain degree of power. The rich know how to use this power, the poor don't.

The author also believes that true luxury is felt when it relates to external manifestations of smart investments and real estate assets. He cites his wife's example, who bought a Mercedes Benz because it was the car she loved and she worked hard to buy it. The author, however, warns of the problems of human frailty in the face of these types of craving or impulse purchases, he recommends making these purchases once the money has been obtained from sales, or assets, so one doesn't go into debt to get them.

Fear, laziness, cynicism and arrogance are the causes of most human inaction.

With this analysis I intend to do my part to help you on your path to success, towards your financial freedom, to become a millionaire, to enjoy life, which is a divine gift.

If you need personal advice, or help on your path to success, feel free to tell me your success story, and don't hesitate to email me at DESPACHOARES@GMAIL.COM

Author of this Analysis. José Sanabria González

Original Book: Rich Dad, Poor Dad. (*Padre Rico, Padre Pobre.*) Robert Kiyosaki

Made in the USA
Middletown, DE
21 February 2023

25300344R00033